Juliet

Doesn't Love You Anymore

Benita Paloja
Illustrator and Editor: Anxhela Spahiu

authorHOUSE®

AuthorHouse™
1663 Liberty Drive
Bloomington, IN 47403
www.authorhouse.com
Phone: 1 (800) 839-8640

Published by AuthorHouse 04/25/2018

ISBN: 978-1-5462-3348-0 (sc)
ISBN: 978-1-5462-3349-7 (e)

Library of Congress Control Number: 2018903383

Print information available on the last page.

Acknowledgments

I would like to acknowledge my family. My parents Adnan and Shpresa Paloja who have supported me throughout this journey. They have been so helpful, understanding, and most of all forgiving to my struggle of becoming the woman I am today. I want to thank them for working so hard to give my sisters and I the life they always dreamed of having but never attained. My mom is the strongest woman I know and my dad is my hero, every single day. They are not only the reason for my existence, but also for my character. I love them more than I can put into words.

I would also like to acknowledge my aunt, Buki. She has been one of the biggest blessings in my young life. Without her, I can honestly say I don't know where I would be. She has always been there to mentor me, to listen to my problems, and has never rejected me in any way. Even though she has got her own little girl now, she will always remain my second mom. I am nothing without her. In addition, my grandmother, Mevlude. I would like to remind her how much we all love and look up to her. She will always have us, and even though that may not always be enough, I pray that it brings her peace knowing she will never be left alone.

A very important acknowledgement must be given to my sisters. Blinera, Bleona, and Eliza Paloja. They are the only ones who know the real me. I truly feel like with them, I can conquer the world. I want to thank them for their loyalty, patience, and attention as I faced the most difficult of times and even the best of times. They pulled me out of the worst spirits and always reminded me of how blessed I was. You all are the reason I gained the courage to write this book. I thank you and love you more than you will ever know.

A sincere thank you goes out to my aunt Fikrije Behrami whom I truly adore. You have always guided

me towards happiness and self worth. For that I am
forever grateful and blessed to have you in my life.
Last but certainly not least I'd like to thank my sisters from
another Mr.'s. Most are living far from me, but remain close to
my heart. I truly thank these girls for genuinely loving me enough
to stick with me at even my worst times. In no particular order, I
must acknowledge; Vildana Bacaliu, Hajrie Gerxhaliu, Anxhela
Spahiu, Kaltrina Sopjani, Kaltrina Hajrizi, Ariana Retkoceri,
Claudia Bajrovic, and Gita Shabani. I appreciate you all.

In Loving Memory of *Jetullah Paloja*

Your shoulders were the safest place I knew. As much as I wish you were around to see who I have become, I am hopeful that you are in a better place watching me from above. I hope you are proud of me. With very little words I want to mention how much I love you and that I will love you forever. You may not be here physically, but you will always live on in our memories. Rest in peace angel.

Me: Are you perfect?

Aga Jetullah: No, nobody is.

Me: So, if no human is perfect, then how do we survive?

Aga Jetullah: *chuckles* The best we can Rrushe, the best we can.

Translated from Albanian

*"Who am I? If you would have asked me
a few months ago I would have said I am
a girl who lets my past strangle me but
never kill me. I did however, let it make me
suffer until my pain exploded onto these
pages. These words are evidence that I let
him take away my sanity, and my certainty.
I saw him clearly, but it was myself that I
could no longer see. I've became a blur..."*

"What are your top 3 fears?", he asked. I squeezed my hands in contemplation, wondering if he was worthy of that knowledge. I began to tell him that losing my eyesight was a big fear. He agreed but wanted more. "Go on", he says. "Losing my parents is another", I explained. "Okay, but what is your *biggest* fear?" I paused, looked into his eyes, "My biggest fear is that the man I love and invest my time in will wake up one morning and realize he no longer loves me." Seconds go by and I refrain from looking at his face; I do not want to see his reaction. Voices in my head whispered doubts: "Maybe that turned him off" circled with "He definitely thinks you're crazy now." What felt like the longest minute of my life ticked by, until I finally gained the courage to lift my head. With his eyes locked on mine, he asks "Why would someone like you fear something like that?" "Well" I started, "that is what always happens. They wake up cold one morning and decide they no longer want their future to begin with me." He frowned and asked, "What do you do to cope with that?" I grabbed a pen and a notebook and told him to sit down next to me. "I'll show you." I began to write the words my soul had etched into the depths of my heart, and when I was finished, his eyes never looked into mine again.

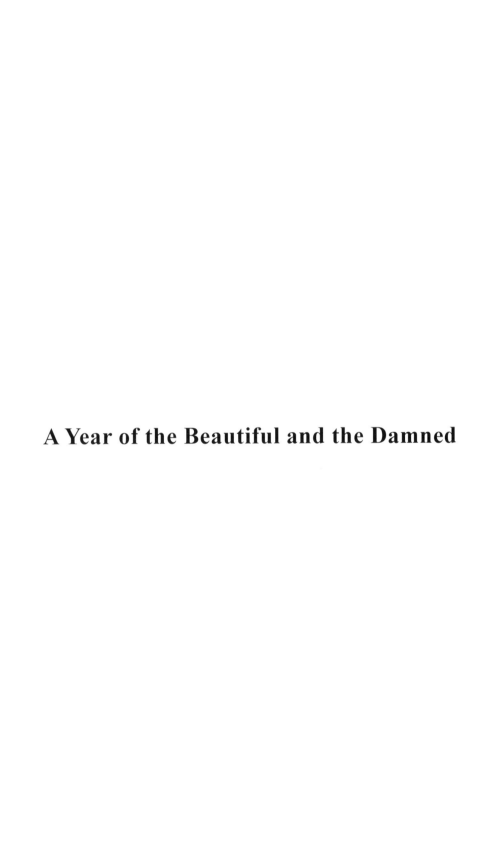

A Year of the Beautiful and the Damned

January

A new year has come around and with it, a new me. Oh, who am I kidding? I'm still the same me, but perhaps a bit more optimistic. I started missing someone new, Mr. New. This year is sure to be it; I can feel it in my bones. My momma is finally going to stop crying, my dad isn't going to worry anymore, and Mr. New will fix all the broken pieces until everything is just right. This feels right, and the beginning of the future I wept for.

February

I stare at a full plate of food and wonder who I am these days. I'm not even hungry. I purposely walk through the freshly fallen snow because something in me is dying to make a mark, any kind of a mark. I'm thinking of a Valentine's Day present that will make him realize that my feelings are real and leave a mark on his heart. But bloody hell, something doesn't feel right.

March

Happy Birthday, Momma. I'm keeping a lot of things from you, but I sense that you still know everything. You are an angel, and I love you. I'm sorry that I am still choosing him, I don't know how to stop. Maybe you can use a candle on your cake to wish for my return, because with him I am definitely a goner. I added him to my list of prayers last night, when I should have been praying for myself. This is the best kind of hopeless.

———————●•O•●———————

April

Something about his arms is addicting. I can't get enough. I crave every inch of him, but he doesn't seem so sure about me. I'm dying inside. So, I took this month to be away from him, hoping he would miss me. I haven't heard from him once. I thought absence made the heart grow fonder? Yet, my absence has only made my heart grow weaker, in constant search for him. He doesn't seem to care. Yet I'm still willing to risk it all for a moment with him. God, damn it! This still doesn't feel right.

May

Cheers to me! Another year older and another year of pretending to be wiser. Now he has decided he missed me, after I have finally convinced myself I don't need him. He's promising me the world and I'm falling for every word he says. I wish I was stronger. You'd think I was starting to learn, but my heart refuses to listen. Last night I pressed my head on his chest and he didn't flinch. Instead, he pulled me in closer. Perhaps my prayers are finally being answered? I feel like I can finally breath again.

June

Why is he doing this to me, again? I don't know why he doesn't love me. He promised me the world but that was the problem, it was HIS world he was offering me. Not one centered on my hopes and desires, not a world where I was the star. More like a tiny background actor that we all see yet never really see, pretending to be happy knowing they didn't make the cut. I'm still not ready to give him up, but I know I need to. I've been sitting in my car outside of his apartment for an hour now. I need to wipe my tears before I walk in and tell him it's over, but they keep falling. Okay, I think I'm ready. Here goes everything I've ever wanted, but nothing I've ever gotten.

July

I find myself on a beach in my homeland with a friend whom I loved like a sister. I'm surrounded by beauty and yet not moved by any of it. I wish he was here. I don't care to see any part of the world, if he's not here to enjoy it with me. Funny how things look so different now that I'm far away from home, far away from him. I miss him so much I almost feel like I would do anything to be with him again. I was blind in love first, and blind from heartbreak now.

August

After spending a summer away, I'm not ready to face him yet. I was hoping that within the peace and serenity of paradise I would also find my backbone, and bring my ego home, too. I know what I bring to the table, I know the kind of love and loyalty I give is rare these days, yet all it takes is the thought of his rejection to make me fold in half. He's my strength and my weakness even when he's not with me.

■•○•■

September

Finally, God has answered my prayers. I swallowed my pride and Mr. Not-So-New is mine again. It feels so good to be wrong this time, to laugh at my insecurities and know that I've won. They say that love always wins, and I'm ready to fight for my happiness. Please let this last, God, please don't let us lose each other again.

October

I should have guessed it would end like this. I thought I had it in me, but I just don't have any fight left to save us this time. Why do I have to rescue him? I'm worth fighting for too, yet every time it's his turn to remind me that I'm the one, he takes a second and that pause shows me that he doesn't get it at all. I'm not stupid, but I have been for him. Congratulations to him, on losing me for good, I hope he never finds what he's searching for.

November

These inner demons of mine have been growing from the pain, whispering to me at night and making me cry as if I were getting paid to drown in tears. Is this real? How do I hurt so much but somehow still want him? The inner devil in me refuses to let go of the pain, perhaps because it is the only tie I've got left to him. Every part of me wonders how I'm breaking while he's okay; no wonder I can't keep the demons away.

December

I wish there was some coming back from this. I wish I could think about the good and laugh off the bad. I wish there was a way to ease the burn of neglect and broken promises and hatred that I feel, even though the hatred barely gets through the disappointment I have in myself for trusting him. Maybe someday, I'll be able to wish him well. Not today though, not right now.

I WILL NEVER STOP MISSING YOU

Dear Heart,

Not only have you taught me how to love, but I never recognized how much I loved you, until I refused to forgive anybody who broke you. You've always been particularly naive when it came to judging people. In which, you always saw the best in them and assumed their love was as sincere as yours is. However, I hope you never lose that quality because it's what makes you so genuine. I realized that God has made you a little too big for my tiny chest. Not that I am judging his work, but the depths of you are a part of me that I haven't discovered yet. I know that in your depths I've let a few people find a home, and as much as we've tried to evacuate some of them, they remain there.

Often, I'm afraid that if you get hurt you again you might close your doors forever. I can't think of anything worse than having a heart in my chest filled with permanent agony and empty promises. I beg of you, take care of yourself because it's clear to see that I don't know how to take care of you.

I wish I could have saved you from myself,

Ms. Sucker for Love

Dear Sleep,

I don't know why you stopped chasing me. I admit that I use you to escape my thoughts. But so, what if I do? If I knew any other way to break free of everything that keeps me up at night, I would choose that instead. For now, you're all I've got.

Perhaps you aren't with me tonight because you're upset. Maybe because I've been choosing him over you for months now. If it makes you feel any better, you aren't the only one I've neglected these past months. I've been choosing him over everyone and everything, including myself. I'm not very good at saying sorry but what I can say is that I wish things were different. Here I go again, overthinking. I need you to rescue me from my mind... please hurry.

Love you madly, need you badly, miss you sadly,

Ms. Sleepless in Boston

Juliet Doesn't Love You Anymore

"Butterflies in my stomach, flying in circles. I feel like I can taste their wings on my tongue. Why do I allow you to do this to me...?"

Love and the City

Our souls attracted one another like a magnet, tugging
our bodies through the city streets and guiding us
towards each other until we finally met eye to eye.
As the rush of the city quieted down, the moon harmoniously
made its way towards the middle of the sky.
Tall buildings towered over us as we walked the streets of the city.
It was a dark, unfamiliar environment but I felt
protected from all the dangers of the broken world.
It was as if the Gods had sent him to me.
Hand in hand, we made our way home.
The feeling was so foreign, yet I had felt it
before, like the sweetest type of Deja Vu.
As we lay on silky white sheets, I stared into his welcoming eyes.
Eyes so full of life, love, and passion.
His hand made his way to my waist and he pulled me in closer.
As I try to memorize the beauty of his existence,
he stares into my eyes deeply.
In his soft, yet strong, voice he says to me, "I am yours."
A rush of emotions flew through my body,
And I then realize that I had loved him before…
in a previous life, too vague to recall clearly.
Yet this I knew: I had never stopped.
I gazed at his perfect face, astonished.
Behind me the world did not exist, because I was
looking at my world, right in front of me.

I Will Always Love You

They say love is blind.
So why were my thoughts becoming clearer
with every perception of you?
Why was my vision improving with every look into
your impeccable brown eyes? I yearn for you.
I crave the taste of your lips and the heat
of your flesh touching mine.
We were two bold souls, but together we effortlessly became one.
We were a force of power too immoral for our human good.
You became my strength and my weakness, a sin
and a blessing that only I could indulge.
With every fiber of my being I idolized you.
Love wasn't enough to describe my passion.
But it was the only word I could think of.
You are a part of me that will live on in my entity
long after I depart from this lifetime.
As my knees become weak and my eyes grew
heavy I whispered," I will always love you."
And I still do.

<u>*Shakespeare*</u>

It seems like the most famous poets wrote about us centuries
before we came into this world.
It's funny,
They somehow knew two souls from two completely different
worlds would come together as one.
They knew how beautifully we would fit together and they also
knew it would never last.
They called it a *tragedy.*
So, it's not our fault that we ruined us.
It had already been written for us to part before we even met.
We tried, but we couldn't cheat destiny.

Words I Never Said to Him

While staring into his hollow eyes deeply,
I'm listening to the words he doesn't say.
I can feel the fire in his heart,
but I also feel the ice through his touch.
It seems like the more we talk, the less we communicate.
The more I reveal my soul to him, the more he keeps me a secret.
I'm living in my own personal Hell, not
knowing which fire will burn less.
With mascara smudged on my pillow case,
I'm wondering when my heart will stop calling him.
I'm caged in my own thoughts while his
mind is lost in a world far from me.
Our relationship was like a ruby red rose with thorns
so sharp they could bring the Devil to his grave.
I guess our fight with destiny only had one outcome all
along, and we were never meant to win that fight.

Yours by Accident

I wake up and stare at his beautiful face sleeping next to me.
I know he's not the one, but at this moment I wish he was.
It pains me to know that his soul is the mate to one that isn't mine.
It frustrates me to think these hands that are holding mine are not
meant to forever... no matter how perfectly they fit together.
These eyes that I see my reflection so clearly in were not
meant to stare into mine for as long as they have.
So, I savor every second as if I would never see him again,
because even though this was never meant to be,
when we're intertwined,
We make destiny rethink why.

<u>*Lost*</u>

If you feel like you have lost your mind, please do not come to me
for help.
I lost mine trying to get into yours.
We both lost. Now, we are both lost.

Dancing with the Devil

She was blindfolded, dancing with the devil.
His smooth feet knew the exact rhythm playing in her brain.
He took her hand and guided her to move in
such ways she never knew she could.
There was something so sexy about the way he tugged and pulled
on her waist, yet she was still free to move as she pleased.
She may have been blindfolded, but she knew damn well
that she was dancing with an immoral being so broken
that he possessed an aura only she could understand.
The wicked creature didn't frighten her;
in fact, he made her feel alive.
In him, she did not see evil. She saw beauty. A magnificence
that was far too distinct for others to capture.
It exposed the way this woman envisioned the world.
She only saw beauty.
The aura that she, too, possessed made her confident
that she could bring even the devil to his knees.
There was one thing she was forgetting, however:
Once the dance ended, and her blindfold was removed,
She would be in hell.

<u>*3am*</u>

I dread you because you always tell me exactly where my
heart is. You filter my thoughts and that's something I'm
trying to avoid now. It's not you, really, it's me. I can't
bear to face the truth about where my heart is right now,
because it's with him. Since he's gone I need to forget, not
remember. I was praying not to run into you again tonight.
It's nothing personal, I just hope we stop meeting like this.

Somewhere Over You, Trying To Get Over You

We were a real-life tale...
Not the kind with horses, fairies, and witches.
More like the kind with drunk kisses and me
tasting cigarettes on your tongue.
Your arms made me feel safe and my
touch made you feel invincible.
Whether attraction, addiction, or passion, I don't
know. Whatever it was, it was strong.
At least until reality began to overpower our feelings.
We were a tragedy masked as a happily-ever after for far too long.
All I wanted was to grow with you,
But all you could do was grow out of me.
I was losing my mind while you were lost in yours.
Red flags became one of my favorite things to ignore,
And I became your favorite thing to forget.
It wasn't long before you became my favorite reason to drink.
As much as I wanted to feel numb, I still held on to a
sliver of the pain because that was all I had left.
And that was enough for me.
Just because I couldn't love you, doesn't mean I didn't.
After all, I was the one who told you to stop playing with fire...
I just didn't expect to be the one who got burnt.

Juliet Doesn't Love You Anymore

I Will Always Be It

With her, everything is simple, and you'll be happy for a little while. You'll kiss her hand while you drive, just like you did with me. You'll tell her jokes and your mom might love her, too. But one day, you will wake up next to her and your bed will still feel empty. She will touch you and you'll feel my fingertips burn your skin in the back of your memory. You'll find that your heart will always be searching for me. The light in her eyes will start to dim because your eyes will stop shining when you see her. You will read every letter she writes to you with my voice echoing in your head. And you will make love to her only in the dark, thinking of my skin pressed against yours. She will begin to live in her own personal Hell, because I will always be the only heaven you know. You see, one day you will finally understand that I was it. She may be what makes sense to you now, but she will never take my place. She will always be a reflection of what you saw in me, carrying the invisible weight of never measuring up, of never being enough. And that will kill her, just like my absence is killing you. I will always be it.

I DON'T FEEL LIKE WRITING ABOUT YOU ANYMORE

Dear Time,

"Koha flet mas miri"

You really fucked me up, you know that? For others, you seem to heal their wounds after a while. They all tell me stories about how everything gets better with time, how time heals all, and how with time blessings come. Though, you never did that for me. My heart still sinks with every thought of any kind of pain I have felt. Maybe I am an exception to that phrase, because my pain was too great for even you to heal. Or maybe I just love harder than most people which is why I can never get over the pain of losing them. If that's the case, then I understand. However, the longer I wait for you to save me; the bigger my wounds have gotten, and they still gush with pain.

I am hoping that someday you will rescue me, and I will know why others love you so much. Until then, I'll expect nothing. Impatiently waiting,

Ms. Girl Who Cried Time

———————◄•○•►

"Silence has more power than words. I learned that from you. I heard from you the most when you stopped hearing from me."

Juliet Doesn't Love You Anymore

*"My plan was to scream my thoughts into this
notebook until the pain was over,
but the only thing that comes after pain is feeling
nothing, and I don't want to be numb.
So, I'll stop right here."*

"I was once so sure I couldn't live without you. The thought of it alone gave me chills and a cold empty feeling. But now, nothing scares me more than the thought of being with you again. You were the reason I felt empty."

Juliet Doesn't Love You Anymore

A Carrie Moment

Fall came back around and so did he.
I bite into a big apple while planning a weekend in New York.
I hear ambulance sirens, which remind me of the city.
I'm thinking space will do me good, with someone
who already gives me too much of it.
Trying to fix us became a hobby I never signed up for.
I was planning my tomorrow with someone
who only saw me as his yesterday,
And I lost more than just sleep.
My reality, too, became a nightmare filled with his
kisses that haunted every inch of my being.
And much like the city, he was exhausting.
I am exhausted.

Heart

I pour wine in my glass as I pour my heart out to you.
I wipe the lipstick off my teeth while you lie through yours.
You hold onto your pride while you should
be holding on to my hand.
I feel my heart shatter instead of feeling butterflies in my stomach.
I taste tears in my mouth instead of your kisses.
I immortalize you with my words while you neglect me with yours.
So here… Let's have a drink for every mountain that we didn't
move. All the things you didn't do right and all the times I
chose to love you anyway. I pray that somewhere between all
the words I failed to say to you, I forgive myself and move on.

Tonight

Tonight,
You're choosing to drink until you're numb.
You're choosing to forget I exist.
You're choosing her over me.
You're turning your phone off, so you can tell me it died.
You're going from one bar to another.
You're searching for happiness in the
world, and not within yourself.
Tonight,
I'm choosing not to text you.
I'm choosing to not break my own heart
while trying to reach yours.
I'm choosing laughter instead of tears.
I'm choosing my happiness over yours.
I'm choosing to sleep instead of worry.
I'm choosing to find my happiness within me, and not within you.

I Am Not Your Answer

My heart grew heavy as your feelings lightened.
My nights become longer as your texts became shorter.
"But you promised." replaced every "I'll be there"
And "What's wrong?" replaced every "I miss you"
Bottle after bottle, my emotions grew number.
So, I kept drinking.
I should have known how this would end from the day
your eyes looked past me when they looked my way.
Maybe you just needed me to prove that it
was possible for you to love again.
Maybe I just needed you to love me the way he didn't.
Maybe this alcohol can help me find an answer.
Or maybe my liver will shut down before it does.
The only clear answer is that I was never yours.
And no matter how loud I scream at you with this poem,
You will never hear me.

<u>Leave Me Alone…. But Please Don't Go.</u>

I didn't want to make this book about you. This is my story, the
one piece of me I no longer wanted you to be a part of. My escape
from you, yet your presence lies between every line. The faster I
turn the page to escape you the more the memory of you bleeds,
leaving ink on my fingertips and staining my resolve.
Leave me alone. You are no longer here, yet you are.
Oh, the irony.
I have officially gone mad. I don't wish
you were here anymore, yet I do.

**This Will Only Make Sense to You**

Everyone wants to marry Happy someday.... momma always told me I belonged with Happy. Yet, I don't know why I'm addicted to Sad. Every night I sneak out to be with Sad, and it's like an addiction that somehow fills the hunger in my heart- and I don't know how to stop wanting. I'm starting to feel like I have problems. but I think I've figured it out; Sad used to make me the happiest girl in the world. Sad used to tell me he wanted to hold me forever. He used to kiss my forehead and let me lay my head on his chest. You see, he wasn't all that bad. Now, all he does is make me sad, but I'm hoping that he can make me happy again, so I hold on to him.

Fuck you

Maybe we're only meant to say fuck you to one another and forget our existence. Maybe that's what our story boils down to… No happy endings, or missing you's, and no letting go of our pride. Can't you see? There is no "forever" with us; just burning passion, fuck you, and goodbye. Fuck you, is our always.

<u>*Searching for Love from a Man*</u>
<u>*Who Doesn't Love Me*</u>

When will my heart stop mentioning you?
When will I stop referring to this poison as love and
start accepting that I don't know what love is?
All I know is that love isn't supposed to hurt,
and every time I look in your eyes, I only feel pain,
And every time I'm with you the night already feels like a memory.
I am desperately waiting for you to teach me how
to love you or teach me how to let you go,
even though I should know better than to search
for love from a man that doesn't love me.

Expire

Had I known we came with an expiration date, I would
have never made everlasting promises with someone only to
spend the rest of forever rotting inside. It's as if I was blinded
by the false promise of eternity by someone with whom
there was no guarantee, except that we would expire.

<u>Daddy, I Should Have Listened</u>

Daddy, I should have listened.
You were right all along…
That boy with bold eyes left me with a broken heart.
My heart was so pure and my love for him was true.
When he told me that he loved me I thought that I did, too.
I was so blind and so afraid I'd lose him,
and every single night it was my heart he was abusing.
He was too damaged, and I thought I could heal him,
but all he did was ruin me and left with part of me missing.
Before I lay to rest, I'm writing you this letter,
Because you've been the only man that cares about me,
and the only man that matters.

<u>*Numb*</u>

I pinched myself today. I just wanted to see if I was still numb.
I was. After you left I felt immense pain and then suddenly, I
felt nothing. It's been two months of nothing. Sometimes I miss
the pain because it was the only thing that l had left of you. I
guess we finally know what the opposite of love is. It's us.

<u>*Regret*</u>

You chose the world over me. Now watch
as I choose myself over you.
Watch me become the woman you always dreamed of having,
Yet I'll be nothing more than a dream to you.
While you remain a nightmare.
I will build myself up with all the words you failed to say,
and I will wish you peace, because I've already found
mine, in all the little pieces you tried to tear me into.

I Don't Mean to Forget You

I'm starting to forget what you smelled like...
Slowly your smile is slipping from my memory.
My fingertips are getting used to not being touched by yours,
And my scent has probably worn off your sheets.
My mouth is starting to forget what your name tastes like,
And my tongue still remembers that your name tasted bitter
I just can't seem to figure out why we let our love sink
when we should have taught ourselves how to swim.

**Red Flags**

Tell me you hate me
Tell me you don't want me.
Whatever you do, please never fall for me.
I don't love people,
I only damage them.
So, don't let me be the girl you ever let in.
My soul is shallow, and heart is black,
My mind races like a psychopath.
"But I love you, just give me a chance"
You don't understand, I just can't.
Forgive me for my detachment,
Excuse me for my harsh words
But don't say you didn't see the red flag,
When you end up burnt.

I Don't

Don't ask me if I miss you, because I don't.
I found beauty in pain once I let you go.
The feelings that were, are now no longer.
The weight is off my shoulders and the horizon seems wider.
The butterflies in my stomach have turned into moths.
The heart you shattered is now yearning to be sought.
I'm capable of loving again,
But not loving you.
Cause my love didn't just walk away,
It flew.

I STARTED MISSING
SOMEONE NEW

June 21, 2017

Dear God,

I seem to be spending a great amount of time doubting you. I mean, I don't aim too. I'm just so mad at you for answering everyone's prayers except for mine. I've been praying for the same thing for the past 6 months and have not heard back from you once. I don't know who I am anymore. I don't understand how you can watch me cry day and night about the same thing and not help me. I have so many questions. Ugh, I was really hoping I could turn to you for this. Please give me a sign.

P.S. I still have faith in you, I just don't like you very much right now. You might not hear from me for a while.

Ms. Falling Apart

Dear God,

I shout, and I shout. Deep down I know that you are answering my prayers every day. I just don't want to believe it because you are not giving me what I want. Every time my situation doesn't change, it's really you telling me I need to let go of what I think I want. Every day he doesn't tell me he loves me is a day that you are telling me to love myself - instead of him. Well today he left me altogether. At first, I thought this was happening because maybe you were answering his prayers of being with someone else, but now I am starting to think that isn't the case. This is really just you answering my prayer to be with someone worthy.

P.S. Thank you for helping me find my way. I'm sorry that I ever doubted you.

Ms. Lost and Found

Dear God,

I now see why you didn't change my situation, it was all because you were trying to change my mind. It took me a while, but I finally understand. I'm now open to all the blessings I have, and I cherish them now more than ever. I'm grateful for every tiny crack in the road of life that you have chosen for me. Who knew that every time I cried in the rain, you stopped the entire storm for me to walk unharmed. All I ever had to do was lift my head up and look beyond the grey clouds: you were always there.

P.S. I'm sorry it took so long for me to see. I will never doubt you again. I hope you can forgive me.

P.P.S. I don't feel lost anymore.
Words aren't enough,

Ms. Faithfully Devoted to You

Dear Dad,

I. Tell me another story, I'm not tired yet.

II. I made you a card, it reads #1 Dad.

III. When I grow up, I want to be just like you!

IV. Are we there yet? I can't believe it's my first day of high school.

V. Am I pretty enough? Why don't boys like me?

VI. I just got my license! Are you proud of me?

...

I. You're wrong about him, he told me he loves me.

II. I can't stand this house. Let me go out. Let me live freely.

III. Your words echo inside my head, I'm sorry I didn't listen.

IV. You were right about him dad; my heart is broken but I still miss him.

V. Thanks for being here. I didn't realize how much you love me.

VI. Can you fix my heart? I don't want to feel anything.

...

I. I realize there is something worse than pain, I just need to numb this feeling.

II. None of this is your fault. You tried to save me, I didn't listen.

III. You don't have to be scared anymore. I'm ready to be free.

IV. I know I don't express it, but you mean so much to me.

V. I just moved in with him. I'll be okay, have no fear.

VI. I'm sorry something came up, Happy Birthday, see you next year!

...

I. Thanks for the flowers dad. It's a girl, I'm so excited!

II. It's been two years since I've seen you. I've been meaning to call you back; I've just been too tired.

III. My daughter called me mommy today, I finally found my purpose in life.

IV. I'm sorry I put you through so much. I now understand why you never gave up.

...

I. I miss you, I miss home.

II. I still need you, please don't ever let me go.

III. Those training wheels I once took off, can you put them back on? This world is rocky, and I don't want to fall.

IV. I miss your smile; I miss your hugs.

V. The real world is mean. I wasn't ready, but I thought I was.

VI. I'm sorry I didn't become who you wanted me to, I know I disappointed you. Although you still love me, I'd do anything for a part two. My heart yearns to be on your shoulders again, that was the safest place I knew. If I could change the clock and rewind time, I'd spend it all with you. As tears rush down my face and onto this letter, I want you to know I'll always be your little girl and I love you, forever.

Ms. Drowning in Regret

To my future daughter,

Baby girl, Mama is going through a breakup that just happened two hours ago. I'm not crying, I feel numb. I don't know why, but right now I don't feel like doing anything other than write this letter to you. You are all I can think about. I'm sitting at a bar next door to my job where I gave my heart to a man who will never be your father. At this moment, all I could so is wish I had a letter like this from my mama. It might have prevented me from consoling my heart at a bar and trying to drown my demons in whiskey.

Let me start by telling you that I am only 22 right now. We have not met and if I'm being honest, I am not ready for you. Although I may never be ready, I know that I will welcome you with loving arms because the day you take your first breath will also be the day I finally know what it feels like to breath. At least, that's what everybody tells me. I'm not going to lie; I've thought of having you ever since I was old enough to know where babies came from.

I need you to keep reading in case you ever go through a breakup that you never think you'll be able to come back from. Just know you're not the first woman to go through what you're going through, nor will you be the last. I always found comfort in knowing I wasn't the first person to experience something bad; hopefully you will too.

Despite my current activities, I need you to know that if you're looking for answers at the bottom of a glass of Henny, you're going to need at least 4 more glasses to numb your pain and by that time, you will see that you're looking for answers in the wrong place. I won't judge you for it though, so don't forget that you can come to me. I've tried drowning every demon I've ever faced in alcohol, but it turns out they all knew how to swim.

The more I think about you the more I wish I could protect you from any kind of pain this broken world offers. Unfortunately, life doesn't work that way. What I can promise you is that I will never judge your decisions; no matter how ugly or how painful. I will always await your arrival with the warmest hugs, and the best lawyers.

Life isn't all that bad though, one day, this world is going to lift you up so high that you will feel invincible; as if you can hold the world in the palm of your hands. And then there will be days when you find yourself stuck between two mountains so big that you won't even feel like you have the power to breathe. I want you to take a moment during both of those times and remember these words.

When you feel like you are too big for the world around you, and begin to feel untouchable, remember that you are not. Also, when you feel small in a world so big it seems it can consume you, know that it can't. The world is as big as you make it, but never stronger, or more powerful than you.

I hope this letter finds you in any moment of weakness you may have, and I hope it serves you. It has taken me 22 years of my life to finally understand that pain is temporary, but mistakes are not. I may have not always had someone to guide me, but you always will. I can't promise you I will always understand your reasoning, but I can promise you that I will always try to. So, whenever you find yourself searching for a sign you can't seem to find; come to me. I will be there to remind you that every worry in your heart can be overcome. I will always love you, and it will always be okay.
Love,

"I hope this book finds you well. Who am I kidding? The only person my words have not found well is me."

I'm Sorry, Mama

I watched you starve just so you could feed me.
I watched you pretend like everything was okay...
I watched your hair turn grey while you lectured me about school
and I never listened.
I watched you pray for your little girl's heart while your little girl
prayed to be as far away from home as possible.
I watched you cry repeatedly because life was never fair to you and
I only made it worse....
Out of all the words I failed to say to you,
I love you was the hardest to keep in, but the hardest to let out.

On my list of regrets, disappointing you is at the top.
I watched you believe women weren't anything more than just a
man's property,
Then I went and dated a boy who treated me that way.
For some reason, I found a comforting feeling in the pain I was
getting from him.
Go figure.
While crying over him, your words echoed inside my head.
"I'm so sorry I didn't listen" is all I remember whispering.

I'll never forget the night I left the house.
I didn't know where I was going,
I cried at just the thought of you not watching me grow up past 19,
but being headstrong was a quality you gave me, so I kept going.
You ran behind me and told me to be safe,
You ran even faster in hopes of me letting you come with me.
I felt your heart crush when I told you to stay and take care of the
girls and I still don't know why you looked over your shoulders to
watch me leave.

Even though at that moment you shouldn't have loved me, you still did. While you paced back and forth not knowing if I would come home to you, I was fighting with myself trying to think of reasons why you still wanted me back.
When I did return, the feeling of your arms wrapped around me again haunted me instead of comforting me.

Regret can ruin even the most tender moment.
I get lost in my thoughts trying to figure out which one of my mistakes disappointed you the most.

The sad part is, I don't think I've made any mistakes that hurt you any less than another.
But I'm now standing at 23, praying to get more than another 23 to make it up to you.
I may not turn out to be the daughter you always wanted,
But I will remind you every day that your happiness means more to me now than mines does.
I'm sorry, mama.

The Quiet to Your Crazy

I'm handcuffed to my past the same way
I'm imprisoned by my thoughts.
I'm yelling at someone who only deserves my silence.
I'm trying to numb the feeling of sadness
while convincing myself it's love.
And I put up with it all because for some reason, I
just wanted to be the peace to your chaos.
But it turns out that you can be everything that
someone needs- until their needs change.

<u>*Addicted to Being Your Contradiction*</u>

I take my sleeping pills with coffee,
Just like I need you, but I hate you.
I tell you I hate you but still pray that you love me.
I'm sick of your lies but I crave every word
that comes out of your mouth.
I'm a contradiction.
But you are no better than me.
You tell me to leave but you follow me out.
Then you tell me to stay but don't make me feel wanted.
I never know where we stand until you're standing in front
of me and I lose control over my sense of control.
And then we're back to square one.

<u>Me After You</u>

Every time I miss you, I tell him that I miss him.
By now I'm sure he's convinced himself he's the man.
Every time I think of you, I tell him to squeeze my hand.
But only to remind myself you're no longer the one holding it.
I close my eyes when he kisses me; sometimes I picture your
lips and bite my tongue before your name slips from my lips.
I give him just enough to keep him around - but
not enough to keep him connected.
There are things I keep sacred and I know it kills him,
I flinch when he tries to cuddle me so that
he doesn't try to touch me anymore.
He doesn't sit next to me when we eat like you did,
he sits across from me and I never complain.
I never leave my things at his place, because I don't
want to remind him I exist, or he might miss me.
And as hard as I try to detach myself from you,
I find myself sleepless next to him,
writing a book about you, and how we almost had it all.

Conflicted

I don't love him... Truth is, I don't even think I like him.
Jesus, I don't even think I like myself most of the time. I
mean, yes, he's in my bed every night but that's only because
the bed is too big for just me. You know, it was meant for
two people, that makes sense, right? I mean since you
can't be here, someone else should. Oh, God, I'm rambling
again. I wish you understood. I wish you were here.

Juliet Doesn't Love You Anymore

Thoughts of a Psychopath

Seconds felt like hours and minutes felt like years.
I told the voice in my head to shut up- she
was giving me a headache.
Pain has found such comfort in my company.
I need to let loose; I need to break free.
If walls could talk, mine would not speak,
Cause my walls have seen Hell,
and watched as the devil laughed at my misery.

<u>Attempting to write about happy</u>

Maybe losing you isn't that bad
Maybe I only make it bad in my mind
Maybe my fears are no bigger than these tears
Maybe they'll disappear with time
Maybe I should have more faith in God, who knows,
Maybe everything I've ever wanted will come after I let you go.

It's Okay

It will rain again, same as it always has. The birds will chirp,
the sun will shine, and the seasons will come and go.
I know you are aware of this, I just wanted you
to know that, yes, I will miss you, but life will
go on without you. And for the first time,
I'm not afraid of it anymore.

His Final Words to Me

"Look me in my eyes and tell me you love me!" I said to him desperately hoping he would give me the answer I was seeking.
"Come on, why is it taking so long to answer? It's been 10 months; you should know by now!" I shouted.
"I feel for you more than I feel for anyone else in a romantic way, so yeah I guess I do love you" he said full of sorrow.

I looked at him surreptitiously relieved at his answer.
"Then why do you have to leave? At least let me come with you, we can tackle this together! I will do anything for you. I'll be whoever you want me to be. Please don't go. Don't break us... Plea..." He then snatched my arm and pulled me close to him.

"I know you would do all of that for me. You are everything I could ever need. There are just too many obstacles we would have to face together, and I don't know if I'm willing to face them with you." his eyes then began to examine mine.
I sat there confused and speechless.
"This isn't your loss. I need to do what's best for me" he looked away.
"But what about me. What about us? I always put us first." I said weeping.

"I don't know. I may regret this for the rest of my life. I can feel myself giving up." he turned his head away from mine.

I continued to sit there in distress. Within a few seconds I grew numb and said to him,
"I don't understand why you're doing this. I trusted you to protect me from all this pain and confusion. Whatever I could do for you, I did. And whatever I couldn't do for you, I tried. You never met me halfway. You led me on for months. You saw all the pain you were causing me, and selfishly, you continued to hurt me. For that, I hope

you DO regret losing me for the rest of your goddamn life because it's clear to see you never deserved me."

I stood up and started heading towards the door. Before I reached the doorknob, I turned around to get one last glance of the man I envisioned forever with.

He took one look at me and with the fear of losing me over-taking his mind, he said, *"So you're not going to fight for us this time?"*

I took a step forward and calmly whispered *"Even though it's hard to imagine a day that I will stop loving you. You have completely drained me emotionally. I don't have any energy left to fight for us. I don't know who I am anymore because of you. And I really don't understand how you could purposely break my heart when all I ever did was love you. I resent you for putting me through this. I do hope you find what you're looking. I hope that all your wildest dreams come true, only for you to realize that they aren't at all what you want. Then, I hope you feel exactly what I have been feeling for you all this time. I hope that one day I look back at you and realize the same exact thing, that you aren't at all what I want."*

I walked out never to return.

A letter to the him that I once knew,

Although writing letters to you has become a tradition of mine, I've been debating on whether this letter would be a good idea or not, and even though I'm still unsure of the answer, I decided to do it anyway. It's hard for me to think of us when there are so many feelings involved and there is no "us" anymore. I know things aren't as black and white as we made them out to be. You now live far from me and yet everywhere I go, I can't seem to escape you.

I'm praying for you even though I should be praying for myself. I read all the letters I almost sent to you before I started writing this one and I'm so happy that they never reached your hands because you didn't deserve them. This letter may have your initials addressed on the outside, but I am writing it to bring myself peace on the inside.

I thought I knew what love was until that cold night in an unfamiliar city when your lips touched mine and every part of me burned on the inside. It wasn't just my lips you kissed- it was my mind, and my heart. I did not know a passion so strong existed and that is why I held on. I mean, how could I ever let that go?

Quite some time has passed since the last time I have seen or spoken to you, but not a second has gone by where you haven't been on my mind. You're so far away, yet so close- but only in my memory of course. It's ironic because while I was with you, it often felt the same way. Almost as if we lost each other long before we really did. We fought to make sense of something that was never supposed to, but hopefully these words bring clarity to you.

"I am giving up" are the only words I seem to remember you by these days. I didn't know words could hurt to the point of physical pain, but they did. After months of fighting for us alone, I didn't have any fight left in me. Then I realized that our love hadn't died that day; our love died the day you picked the world over me. Our love died the day you picked her over me. Our love died the day that you decided your future included a fresh start without me while I fought endlessly to make sure that my future always started with you. I'm starting to think I don't know the real meaning of love, but I sure as hell know that what I felt for you was greater than any love story ever written.

Though it has taken me a few months, I finally can wish you well. I may have pushed too hard or held on too tight, who knows. I had to let go of us and accept that your arms will no longer be the ones I crawl into after a long day and my fingers will no longer be the ones that linger on your neck while you rest your head on my chest. I had to accept that my everything wasn't enough, and that another woman will effortlessly get the best versions of you while I drained myself in every way possible to get even the most insignificant bits. I had to accept that I was nothing but a convenience to you and a pretty distraction from the reality you weren't ready to face. Most difficult of all, I had to accept every tear, and every 3 am I spent mourning us.

Regardless of my reflections on everything "we" meant to me, this is not a love letter to you. I'm not that girl anymore. I want you to know that I hated who I was when I was with you. I hated that I so desperately loved you and was always trying to change myself into the woman you couldn't stop yourself from marrying someday. I tried to open my heart, mind and soul- just for you- so you'd have a dream of seeing me walk down the aisle in a moment that only exists in movies, where your eyes light up when you see me, and your mom would cry tears of joy because even though she didn't like me she loved how happy I made you. By the way, I never liked your brother's girlfriend who always reminded me that I wasn't good enough for your family because I didn't have as much money and freedom as she did. Most of all, I absolutely HATED that I felt so used the day you told me you had decided to start a life without me without even asking me how I would feel or to come along with you. You said you loved me, but you weren't willing to overcome the obstacles life was going to throw our way. You gave up, and people don't give up on someone they love.

I was a hopeless romantic in love with a man that was full of empty promises, *un-meaningful* kisses, and an uncanny way of making me believe the lie that we stood a chance against the world. For so long, I really believed we did. Who would have guessed that you would have been the one to break us? Who would have guessed that the biggest hurdle we faced was that your heart was a little too hard to find and I grew weak searching for it?

But despite how things ended between us, I want to thank you for the past year. It has been one of the best and the worst years of my life, all at the same time. I will never forget our time in your hometown and feeling so lucky to be yours. My birthday, where I could see our future in your eyes and you spent the night telling me I never had to worry because you were entirely mine. Best of all, all the date nights that only you and I will ever understand the passion behind. I'll miss every laugh we shared, right up until our story ended. Luckily, mine is just beginning, and I thank you for the lessons that made me a force to be reckoned with. Today, I'm a woman who knows her worth, crowned in her own glory and capable of loving again while keeping herself first. Juliet doesn't kill for love anymore, not in this story.

With NO love,

The Her You Once Knew

Juliet Doesn't Love You Anymore

MIRESEVJEN NE SHPIRTIN TIM

Botën Nga Sytë e Tu

(Kam pa botën në sytë e tu dhe nga ai moment,
s'mund ta shoh askend në sy)
Një njeri më quajti Zemër,
Unë nuk e njoha aspak...
Më kapi dorën dhe tha "Eja me mua,
Kam një botë për ta treguar."
Unë e hutuar vrapova pas tij,
Dhe arritëm te një shkëmb, ku u ul ai.
"Ku na qenka kjo botë tjetër,
Unë vetëm pemë shikoj tani?!"
Më tha "a nuk e sheh?
Botën shikoje në sytë e mi…"

Një Gotë Për Ty

Gotë pas gote, prap mendjen tek ti.
Si na erdhi dita, që s'do shihemi përsëri.
Mëngjeset me shpresa, dhe netët me gënjeshtra.
Të duroja, sepse të deshta.
Unë ja bëja qefin vetes,
mendoja se më doje ti.
Faji mbet tek ajo natë,
që u ndamë ne të dy.

Shpresa vdes e fundit,
dhe unë do vdes para sajë
se dhimbjen, që kam brënda,
më nuk mundem ta mbajë.
Sa u dëshprova unë,
Vetëm Zoti e din.
Ndoshta një ditë e kupton,
Sa shumë ishe gabim.

Pas Teje, Gjdo Gjë U Bë Akull

Vetëm ate e doja shumë, po ai nuk besonte në dashuri
E kisha zemrën të pastër dhe të plotë.
E doja atë aq shumë që çdo natë përballoja lotë.
Gjithmonë e dëshpruar sepse ai nuk më vlersoi,
Unë lutesha për mrekulli dhe asgjë nuk ndryshoi.
Plagët i mbylla me dhimbje kurse shenjat me pikllime,
Tash vetëm zbrazëti më mbeti në kujtime.
Ç'dreq do ai në mendjen time?!
Gabimet nuk mund t'ia fal...
Me çfar fytyre më flet ky përsëri?!
Nuk dua ta njoh më aspak.
Nxehtësia e zemrës time u bë akull tani.
Dashuria sjell lotë...
Po jo lotë të palumturisë.

<u>Ditlindja Jote pa Mua</u>

Sa planet i kemë pasë,
sa dashninë ta kam dhënë!...
Erdhi dita me pritë ditlindjen tënde pa mua.
Sa deshirat i kemë pasë,
sa yjet i kemë numrua,
sot nuk mundem të tregoj sa të dua.
Jeta qenka e hidhur,
dhe faji mbeti jetim,
Po zemra, që të deshti, do të mban ty në kujtim.

Ike ti, si ëndërr
Unë vrapova, po ti u zhduke.
S'kam menduar asnjëherë,
Që kam fuqi të vazhdoj tutje.
Çdo natë shikoja hënën,
Dhe kam pasur vetëm një lutje,
Që t'më duash ti sa ç'të dua unë,
Dhe t'më pranosh kështu siç mund.

Si mund ti sjellësh jetë lotëve t'mi,
Dhe të vazhdosh me jetën tënde?!
Dua të jem një ditë pa ty,
Dhe t'mos ndjeja asnjë dhimbje.
Kjo thikë me dy teha të mpreht,
Veç dhimbje mund t'na sjell
Dhe çdo ditë vazhdojmë ta mprehim,
Dhe t'ia fiksojmë njeri-tjetrit në zemër.
S'kam durim të të flas më,
Por s'mund t'jetoj pa fjalët e tua.
S'kam besim tek ne më,
Por çdo natë lutem që t'jeshë me mua.

"Ndoshta lote mund të lehtësojë dhimbjen,
Por ata nuk kanë fuqi për të gjetur ty.
Tani vetëm në kujtime,
Ti përjetësisht qëndroni tani."

Juliet Doesn't Love You Anymore

"... Who am I? If you ask me now. I'll tell you that my past and I have cut all ties. My demons and I no longer speak, and I will bleed strength before I ever allow my sanity to abandon me again."

**Biography**

Benita Paloja also known as Rrushe, Bita, and Bena, was born on May 13, 1995 in Pristina, Kosovo. In 1999, Benita and her family journeyed to the USA as a result of the Balkan War. The author along with her three younger sisters and parents now reside in Boston, MA. Aside from writing, she also has a thriving career in marketing that feeds her desire to travel, as well as in public relations that feeds her love of meeting and communicating with a vast variety of people. With this, she also is mastering her degree in Psychology and Communications.

Benita began writing at the age of 13, however, did not begin to share her poems until the age of 17. She turns to writing in good times and in bad as an escape from reality as well as for personal therapy. In her own words, she states that: _"I hope that one day, a girl who is praying to God for a sign, finds my book. I hope that she reads it and it helps her with whatever obstacle she thinks she wont be able to overcome. I wish I had something like this to read when I thought I would never survive what I was going through. This book is for her."_

She also emphasizes her ambition to make the Albanian Community more known to the world. _"I am Kosovar/Albanian before I am anything else, my biggest goals apart from making my family proud is to raise awareness to outside cultures about how much beauty and pain lies within the Albanian streets and behind every Albanian's eyes."_

To conclude, Benita's final words are _"I may not have walked this earth for a very long time, however, I have been faced with situations that not many would be able to come back from. Nonetheless, growing consists of escaping comfort zones, making mistakes, and learning to water my own grass instead of dreaming of greener grass. I spent a great deal of time holding onto anger, grudges, pride, and doubt._

Only to then realize that my best friends are humility, strength, and resilience. 2017 may have been the year of questions for me, but the years to come will be the years of answers. I look forward to sharing my journey with you all through my writings."

Printed in the United States
By Bookmasters